Lee Bailey's TOMATOES

by Lee Bailey

Photographs by Tom Eckerle

CLARKSON POTTER/PUBLISHERS
NEW YORK

Published by Clarkson Potter/Publishers, 201 East 50th Street, New York, New York 10022. Member of the Crown Publishing Group.

CLARKSON N. POTTER, POTTER and colophon are trademarks of Clarkson N. Potter, Inc.

Manufactured in Japan
Design by Howard Klein
Library of Congress
Cataloging-in-Publication Data

Bailey, Lee.
    [Tomatoes]
    Lee Bailey's tomatoes / by Lee Bailey ; photographs by Tom
Eckerle. — 1st ed.
        p.   cm.
    1. Cookery (Tomatoes)   I. Title.
TX803.T6B33   1992
641.6'5642—dc20   91-32741
                                                          CIP

ISBN 0-517-58809-9
10 9 8 7 6 5 4 3 2

A while ago, my old friend Florence Fink said, "Lee, why don't you do a little book about tomatoes for me." Okay, Florence, here it is! With love, too.

Thanks to Jane and Stewart Maunsell II, Ruth Mitchell, and Florence Klotz for letting me photograph at their houses. And thanks to Tom Eckerle for his lovely pictures and to Lee Klein for his help.

As usual, my appreciation to all the folks at Clarkson Potter and to Pam.

To tell you the truth, I've never been too sure about love at first sight. *Lust* at first sight, sure—but love at first sight, I just don't know. But I *do* know that with me and tomatoes it was love at first bite. And the affair has been going on for more years than I care to count.

I can recall a specific occasion from the tender age of seven when my romance with tomatoes was already in full flower. I've told about it before, but I do want to share it again here.

After my maternal grandfather died, Mawmaw—my grandmother—moved from Argyle Plantation (where I was born) to "town," a community of about two thousand. This was Melville, on the Atchafalaya River in south-central Louisiana. In those days Melville was on the principal route to

New Orleans, two hundred miles to the south. At Melville automobiles had to cross the river by ferry before going on down to the Crescent City. There was also a train bridge; the tracks that led up to it had been laid along the top of a levee that surrounded the town.

Number 24, the train to New Orleans, passed through Bunkie, which was thirty miles up the line from Melville and where I lived with my parents. By the time I was seven I was allowed to take the Number 24 down to Mawmaw's house by myself. Between Bunkie and Melville there were four stops—not exactly a bullet train, but there was lots of bustle (it seemed to me) and plenty to see. The same conductor and porters were always on board, and they made sure I got off where I was supposed to. They all recognized Parson, who never failed to meet me at the Melville depot with Miss Woo, a great white dog, at his side. Parson was about as old as a person can be and still look like a person. He had only one arm and—as unreal as it is for me to remember now—he had

been born into slavery. Parson had worked for my grandfather's family for almost sixty years, so when my grandmother moved he came along and was given a little house in the far corner of her sprawling garden in which to live out his days.

Anyway, the two of us would walk back to the house with Miss Woo running ahead and circling around us. The only person she really loved and had any respect for was Parson, who was so skinny she could have knocked him over in a minute. But when he called out to Miss Woo, or scolded her in his hoarse crackle, she would mind, returning beseechingly with her head down to receive his forgiveness for her sins of boisterousness.

My grandmother, on the other hand, was too stern for Miss Woo's tastes, and, being a woman content with her settled state, had very little patience with M.W.'s unseemly girlish enthusiasm and foolishness. I once heard Mawmaw remark, "That grown dog is so silly, she thinks she's still a puppy."

Through the dew-covered bitterweed we'd go, as I chattered on about my train-ride adventures, to where my grandmother waited. She had long ago realized—most sensibly—that I was the most marvelous grandchild a person could ever wish for. After lots of kissing and hugging and having my still almost-white hair smoothed (I was known as—what else?—"Cotton Top"), I'd be told to go out into the garden to pick the best, reddest, ripest tomato I could find. By the time I got back, lunch would be ready. You see, my grandmother knew that although it was just barely ten in the morning, her darling would be exhausted and famished after such an arduous journey.

Lunch consisted of my favorite things: tomatoes with home-made mayonnaise (my most prized food in the world), popcorn, iced tea, and watermelon for dessert. This Mawmaw unflinchingly ate as though she had just arrived along with me, starved after the same hair-raising trip, and famished for *her* favorite meal.

So you see—there it is, plain as day. The thing had already taken hold, and I was still years from being out of short pants.

But I know I'm not alone in this infatuation. There are enough tomato lovers out there to make the Elvis and Jackson (Michael *and* Bo) fan clubs look slim.

I have a theory about what gives the tomato its ability to keep on bewitching. You know how in magazines there are articles about how to put the zip back into your marital sex? And how, after all the fuss about surprising (or scaring) the wits out of your partner, these articles sometimes get around to the surefire way—absence? I suspect tomatoes knew this all along, because they *really* aren't their succulent selves any time of the year except when they can be eaten vine-ripened. Forget the attempts to get them to us out of season. At best, these only provide us with a pale reminder of what we're missing—and what we have to look forward to. And, oh, when they return. It's a honeymoon all over again.

The little rascals aren't known as love apples for nothin'.

Recipes

———◆———

FRESH TOMATO ASPIC

———◆———

I'd wager there's not a soul from the Deep South who didn't grow up with tomato aspic. Whether you loved it or could leave it alone, it was always there. I love it, but I never seem to have it these days. I vow to change if you'll take the vow, too.

3 pounds tomatoes
1 medium green bell pepper, seeded and grated
1 medium onion, grated
1½ teaspoons salt
½ teaspoon black pepper
3 tablespoons Worcestershire sauce
2 teaspoons Tabasco sauce
3 tablespoons fresh lemon juice
3 envelopes unflavored gelatin soaked in ¾ cup water

Peel and seed the tomatoes, saving the juice. Chop enough into small dice to make 1 cup. Puree the rest, and add enough of the reserved juice to make 3½ cups. (If short, add a little canned tomato juice.)

Combine the diced tomato, bell pepper, onion, salt, black pepper, Worcestershire, Tabasco, and lemon juice. Set aside.

In a small saucepan, warm the puree over low heat. Stir in the softened gelatin and stir to dissolve. Add the reserved diced-tomato mixture and taste for seasoning. Pour into a 6-cup mold and refrigerate for several hours, until set.

To unmold, place the mold in a pan of hot water long enough to loosen the edges, cover with a serving plate, and invert. Return to the refrigerator for 15 to 20 minutes, then serve.

Serves 8 or more

TOMATO SPOON BREAD

If you have a favorite spoon bread recipe, use it. Simply add to it the amount of tomatoes called for here. This version produces a very stable, corn bread–like spoon bread.

> *2 cups milk*
> *2 eggs*
> *2 tablespoons unsalted butter*
> *⅔ cup white cornmeal*
> *1 teaspoon salt*
> *2 teaspoons sugar (optional)*
> *2 teaspoons baking powder*
> *4 to 6 tablespoons coarsely chopped Oven*
> *"Sun-Dried" Tomatoes (page 31)*

Preheat the oven to 450 degrees and generously butter a 1½-quart soufflé dish.

Combine ⅔ cup of milk with the eggs and beat well. Set aside. Combine the remaining milk and the butter in a saucepan over low heat. Bring just to a simmer. Over slightly increased heat, add the cornmeal in a steady stream, stirring constantly. Stir in the salt and sugar. Off the heat, add the milk mixture, whisking until smooth. Sprinkle the baking powder over all, and whisk to combine. Stir in the tomatoes. Pour into the soufflé dish, and bake until puffy and golden, about 30 minutes. Serve immediately.

Serves 6

TOMATO GOUGERE

People who have never made or had this bread are amazed when they discover how uncomplicated it is to prepare. Delicious and impressive for a cocktail party!

> *2 ounces Oven "Sun-Dried" Tomatoes (page 31)*
> *1 cup water*
> *½ cup (1 stick) unsalted butter*
> *Pinch of salt*
> *1 cup sifted all-purpose flour*
> *4 eggs, at room temperature*
> *4 ounces Gruyère cheese, cut into small dice*
> *(about ⅔ cup)*

Preheat the oven to 425 degrees and grease a baking sheet.

Cover the tomatoes with hot water and allow to soak for about 10 minutes. Drain, dry, and chop fine. Set aside.

Put the water, butter, and salt in a saucepan. Bring to a boil. Dump in the flour all at once and stir vigorously over medium heat until the paste begins to pull away from the sides of the pan. Off the heat, beat in the eggs, one at a time. Stir in the tomatoes and cheese.

Place heaping tablespoons of dough just touching in a small circle on the baking sheet. Keep adding to the outside of the circle until all of the dough is used. Bake for 10 minutes and turn the heat down to 350 degrees. Continue to bake until golden, about 20 more minutes. Serve warm.

Serves 6 to 12

TOMATO BREAD PUDDING

———◆———

Bet you never had this before. I hadn't either until a couple of years ago. You'll like it with ham or chicken (or maybe both together), or at room temperature with a salad and cheese for lunch. White Italian bread with a thick crust is best for this.

> *3 large tomatoes, peeled*
> *About 10 slices white Italian peasant bread,*
>   *toasted*
> *4 tablespoons mild olive oil*
> *³/₄ to 1 teaspoon salt*
> *1 teaspoon dried parsley*
> *¹/₂ teaspoon dried tarragon*
> *¹/₂ teaspoon sugar*
> *Black pepper to taste*
> *4 generous tablespoons freshly grated*
>   *Parmesan cheese*
> *2 English muffins, split and toasted*

Preheat the oven to 350 degrees and generously butter an 8-inch soufflé dish.

Cut the tops and bottoms off the tomatoes to even them; save the extra pieces. Cut each tomato into 2 equally thick slices. Line the bottom of the soufflé dish with the bread, cutting a slice into pieces to patch with so as to loosely cover the whole bottom. Place half the tomato slices on top, filling in spaces with half the extra tomato pieces. Drizzle half the olive oil over the tomatoes, then sprinkle with half the salt, parsley, tarragon, and sugar. Add a grind of black pepper. Make another layer of bread, and top with the remaining tomato slices and pieces. Add oil and seasonings as before. Sprinkle with the Parmesan cheese.

Tear the English muffins into large pieces and put in a food processor. Process into large crumbs and sprinkle on top.

Bake, uncovered, for 40 to 45 minutes. Cover with foil and bake another 30 minutes, until the tomatoes are soft and the bread has a puddinglike texture. If you like, drizzle some olive oil on individual servings.

Serves 6 to 8

BAKED TOMATOES STUFFED WITH ANDOUILLE SAUSAGE AND RICE

Stuffed tomatoes are sometimes dry, so bake them with a little broth in the pan. The juices can be spooned over the tomatoes when they're served. These are good hot or at room temperature. You may substitute any spicy smoked sausage for the andouille.

TOMATO SHELLS

4 large tomatoes
Salt and black pepper to taste
2 teaspoons olive oil
¼ teaspoon Tabasco sauce
1 teaspoon minced garlic (optional)

FILLING

2 tablespoons olive oil
½ cup finely diced onion
½ cup finely diced yellow bell pepper
½ pound andouille sausage, finely chopped
1 cup cooked rice
2 tablespoons chopped fresh parsley
¼ teaspoon black pepper
3 tablespoons fresh bread crumbs
1 tablespoon unsalted butter
¼ cup chicken stock

Prepare the tomato shells: Hollow out the tomatoes from the stem end. Discard the seeds and chop the pulp. Set the pulp aside for the filling.

Invert the shells on a rack and drain for 10 to 15 minutes. Sprinkle the insides with salt and pepper, then rub them with a mixture of the oil, Tabasco, and garlic. Place hollowed side up in a greased gratin dish.

Preheat the oven to 375 degrees.

Make the filling: Heat the oil over medium-high heat and sauté the onion, stirring, for 2 minutes. Add the bell pepper and sausage. Cook for 3 minutes longer. Stir in the reserved tomato pulp and cook for another minute or so. Off the heat, stir in the rice, parsley, and black pepper (the sausage adds enough salt). Correct the seasoning. Spoon the filling into the tomato shells. Top each with bread crumbs and a bit of butter. Pour the broth into the dish. Bake for 25 to 30 minutes, until the tops are light golden and the skins start to shrivel. Spoon juices over all when serving.

Serves 4

OMATO CENTERPIECES

This is how you can get double duty out of your tomatoes: one day they're a centerpiece, and the next a salad.

The best way to tell you how to use tomatoes as a centerpiece is to say, "Look at these photographs." You can combine colors of tomatoes, make pyramids of them, and add sprigs of green. In all cases, it's obviously important to find the best specimens, and when arranging them to find ones that are of a consistent size. Of course, neatness is important. . . . If you have trouble keeping the whole thing together, you might use toothpicks to hold the tomatoes in place, but that usually isn't necessary.

Think about a centerpiece of small baskets of mixed yellow and red cherry tomatoes combined with leaves—or even small bunches of flowers. Or you could go all the way and simply plunk down a big low-sided basket piled high with tomatoes right out of the garden—some with stems still attached.

I don't know if others share this quirk, but I especially like the aroma tomato leaves give off when you handle them. Leaving a few leaves on the stems adds this fresh summer scent to the table.

What I like today is a pretty far cry from the cream of tomato soup of my childhood.

COLD ROASTED TOMATO AND SWEET RED PEPPER SOUP

—————◆—————

I always keep a batch of this in my refrigerator during the summer. One taste is all you need to be converted.

> *2½ pounds ripe tomatoes*
> *2 large red bell peppers (about ¾ pound)*
> *1 tablespoon unsalted butter*
> *½ pound onions, coarsely chopped*
> *½ celery rib, coarsely chopped*
> *1 small carrot, grated*
> *4 cups rich chicken stock*
> *Salt and white pepper to taste*
> *Sour cream or crème fraîche*

Put the tomatoes in a low-sided baking pan and set them under the broiler. Roast them as you would peppers, turning with tongs until the skins blacken, about 5 minutes. Transfer them to a plate and set aside. They will give up quite a bit of liquid as they cool; drain it off and discard it. Peel the tomatoes and cut out the stem ends.

Roast the bell peppers as you did the tomatoes. When they are blackened, put them in a small bag and close it. Set aside.

Put the butter, onions, celery, and carrot in a saucepan with a tablespoon or two of the stock. Shaking the pan to prevent sticking, simmer, covered, over low heat for 10 minutes, until the vegetables are soft but not browned. Add the tomatoes and simmer, covered, for 15 minutes. Stir occasionally to prevent scorching.

Dump this all into a strainer or food mill and mash the solids through to get rid of the seeds. (A few whirls in a food processor before straining speeds this step up.) Return the strained pulp to the saucepan and add the chicken stock. Simmer, uncovered, for 30 minutes, skimming.

Peel, seed, and puree the peppers. Add to the saucepan and simmer for just a few more minutes. Let cool. Correct the seasoning with salt and pepper, if necessary. Serve chilled with a large spoonful of sour cream or crème fraîche on top.

Serves 4 to 6

HOT TOMATO AND RICE SOUP WITH SAUSAGE BALLS

If you would like to freeze this, leave out the rice and sausage.
Add them when you serve it.

> **1 tablespoon unsalted butter**
> **½ pound onions, coarsely chopped**
> **¼ celery rib, coarsely chopped**
> **1 small carrot, grated**
> **4 cups rich chicken stock**
> **2¼ pounds ripe tomatoes, roasted (page 26)**
> **1 tablespoon minced fresh parsley**
> **2 tablespoons minced fresh chervil**
> **Salt and black pepper to taste**
> **2 tablespoons uncooked long-grain rice**
> **½ to ¾ pound sausage meat**

In a saucepan, combine the butter, onions, celery, and carrot
with 1 cup of the chicken stock and simmer, covered, over low
heat for 10 minutes. Add the rest of the stock.

Peel the blackened skin from the tomatoes, and drain off any
juice. Add the tomatoes to the saucepan, cover, and simmer
over low heat for another 15 minutes, stirring occasionally.

Puree the mixture briefly in a food processor and then put it
through a strainer or food mill. Discard the seeds and return
the puree to the saucepan. Add the parsley, chervil, and salt
and pepper. Bring to a simmer and add the rice. Simmer for 10
minutes, or until the rice is tender.

Meanwhile, roll the sausage meat into walnut-sized balls.
Brown them and add them to individual servings of the soup.

Serves 6

Here are some of the best things you can do with tomatoes, besides eating them right off the vine. The first is smoking—a process that's simple but gives delicious results and forms the basis for a marvelous sauce (page 37). Another is oven curing—cooking whole tomatoes in a very slow oven until they collapse and their flavor is concentrated.

SMOKED TOMATOES

This method comes from chef Gerard Maras at Mr. B's Restaurant in New Orleans.

If you have a smoker, follow the directions to prepare it for smoking. You can also use a charcoal grill with a cover—such as a Weber—and get a medium-sized charcoal fire going.

Prepare about 3 pounds of tomatoes for smoking. With a melon baller, core out the stem end of each tomato. With a sharp knife, make an X incision in the other end.

When the coals have burned to where they are covered with white ash, sprinkle moistened chips (hickory, mesquite, pecan, grape cuttings) over them to produce a heavy smoke. Place the tomatoes on an oiled grill, X side down. Replace the cover and adjust the vents to an almost-closed position; the coals should smoke but not flame up.

The smoking process should take anywhere from 45 minutes to 1 hour. Check the tomatoes shortly after putting them on to make sure your fire is not too hot. If they seem to be cooking, add more moistened wood chips to cool the fire down. The tomatoes are ready when they are very soft but retain their basic shape. The skins will be splitting and the tomatoes a bit wrinkled; the cored end will be full of liquid. You want to save all the juices, so keep the tomatoes upright as you transfer them to a colander placed over a bowl. When they are cool enough to handle, slip off the skins and separate the seeds from the pulp. Reserve the pulp and juice and discard the skins and seeds. Use the smoked pulp to make any sort of sauce. The one on page 37 is an example—and it's terrific.

Incidentally, you might measure how much juice and pulp these 3 pounds of tomatoes produce, because that's the quantity called for in the sauce recipe, and you might want to smoke larger quantities.

OVEN ''SUN-DRIED'' TOMATOES

This is how you can "sun-dry" tomatoes in the privacy of your own kitchen. Maybe they aren't Tuscan, but then how many of us are? And besides tossing 'em in with your pasta, you can use them to make Tomato Spoon Bread (page 15) or Tomato Gougère (page 16).

Set your oven to its lowest, below 200 degrees. Slice Italian-style (Roma or plum) tomatoes in half, top to bottom. Scoop out the seeds with your fingers. Place, cut side down, directly on the oven racks and let them dry out for 12 to 15 hours. I usually put them in when I go to bed and let them go all night.

OVEN-CURED TOMATOES

———◆———

This method comes from Larkin Selman, chef/owner of Gautreau's Restaurant in New Orleans. Use these tomatoes in everything from composed salads to vinaigrettes.

> *6 medium tomatoes (about 3 pounds)*
> *1 tablespoon minced garlic*
> *1 tablespoon chopped fresh thyme*
> *2 tablespoons olive oil*
> *¼ teaspoon salt*
> *¼ teaspoon black pepper*

Core the stem end of the tomatoes and cut an X in the bottom. Dip in boiling water for 8 to 10 seconds, then immediately into ice water. Slip the skins off and cut each tomato in half crosswise.

Line a sheet pan with foil and lightly oil it. Place the tomatoes on the foil, cut side down. Combine the remaining ingredients and rub each tomato half with the mixture.

Place in the oven and turn it to 225 degrees. Bake for 5 hours, until the tomatoes are soft but retain their shape. To store, cover with olive oil and refrigerate them.

Easy to make and delicious, these sauces can be used as they are or as the basis for many variations. I like the all-purpose sauce tossed with pasta and topped with grilled vegetables. But how about mixing in roasted and pureed red bell peppers? Or tuna fish, black olives, and capers? Almost anything goes.

ALL-PURPOSE TOMATO SAUCE

You can use canned tomatoes here—if you must.

> *¼ cup olive oil*
> *3 cups chopped onions*
> *1¾ to 2 cups shredded carrots*
> *1 heaping tablespoon minced garlic*
> *12 cups peeled, seeded, and coarsely chopped*
> *   tomatoes (with any juice)*
> *2½ teaspoons salt, or to taste*
> *1 teaspoon black pepper*
> *1 tablespoon minced fresh basil*

Heat the oil in a deep pot and sauté the onions and carrots over medium-high heat until wilted, 4 to 5 minutes. Stir in the garlic. Add the tomatoes and bring to a simmer. Stir in the salt, pepper, and basil. Simmer to reduce and thicken, about 10 to 15 minutes. Do not overcook.

Transfer to a food processor and process just enough to make a coarse texture.

Makes about 12 cups

UNCOOKED TOMATO SAUCE

———◆———

You have to let your own taste buds be your guide here. When you toss this together, add the smaller amounts of vinegar and oil, a little salt and pepper, and a dash of Tabasco if you like. Taste and go on from there.

> *6 medium to large tomatoes, cut into large*
>   *chunks*
> *1 small garlic clove, minced*
> *1 tablespoon minced shallot*
> *½ medium onion, chopped*
> *3 tablespoons coarsely chopped fresh basil*
> *3 to 4 tablespoons balsamic vinegar*
> *6 to 8 tablespoons olive oil*
> *Salt and black pepper to taste*
> *Tabasco sauce to taste (optional)*

Drain off and discard any liquid from the tomatoes. Mix the tomatoes with all of the remaining ingredients. Let the mixture stand at room temperature for about 20 minutes. Toss with hot pasta and top with grated Romano or Parmesan cheese.

Makes about 8 cups

SMOKED TOMATO SAUCE

Here's another recipe from Gerard Maras at Mr. B's. This sauce is especially good on angel hair pasta.

> **3 pounds Smoked Tomatoes, peeled and seeded (page 30)**
> **1½ teaspoons chopped fresh thyme**
> **1½ medium bay leaves**
> **¼ teaspoon dried oregano**
> **¼ teaspoon dried marjoram**
> **1 tablespoon paprika**
> **1 teaspoon minced garlic**
> **Pinch of crushed red pepper**
> **¼ cup rich chicken stock**
> **2 tablespoons rice vinegar**
> **¼ cup heavy cream**
> **4 tablespoons unsalted butter, softened**
> **Romano cheese to taste**

Put the tomatoes in a saucepan over medium heat. Add the herbs and spices. Simmer for 6 to 8 minutes, stirring occasionally. Remove from the heat. Discard the bay leaves. Puree the mixture in a food processor. Return it to the heat and stir in the stock and vinegar. Bring to a boil, turn the heat down, and simmer for another 6 to 8 minutes to thicken the sauce.

To finish the sauce, add the cream and reheat. Off the heat, beat in the butter. Correct the seasoning if necessary, and toss with freshly cooked pasta. Top with shaved curls (use a vegetable peeler) of Romano.

Makes enough for 1 pound of pasta

Both these delights, brothers under the skin, fall into the category of what I call "reward food"—which I define as something you could continue eating after you are finished eating.

SAVORY TOMATO PIE

————◆————

Made basically with biscuit dough, this is Roy Finamore's—my editor—famous tasty and simple treat.

PASTRY

2 cups flour
½ teaspoon salt
2 teaspoons baking powder
½ cup (1 stick) unsalted butter, chilled and cut into small pieces
⅔ cup milk

FILLING

3 pounds ripe tomatoes, peeled, seeded, and sliced thick
2 tablespoons chopped fresh chives
3 tablespoons chopped fresh basil
¾ teaspoon salt
¼ pound sharp white cheddar cheese, grated
⅔ cup mayonnaise

Preheat the oven to 400 degrees.

Make the pastry: Sift the dry ingredients together and cut in the butter with a pastry blender or two knives until the butter pieces are the size of small peas. Stir in the milk. Turn out on a floured board and knead a few times. Divide in two and roll out half. Line a 10-inch pie pan with one half and set aside.

Make the filling: Mix the tomatoes, herbs, salt, and half the cheese. Spoon into the pie pan. Spread with the mayonnaise, and sprinkle the balance of the cheese over all. Roll out the remaining dough and cover the top, sealing around the edges. Bake until golden, about 20 to 25 minutes.

Serve warm. The pie may be reheated.

Serves 6 to 8

TOMATO TARRAGON PIZZA

———◆———

If you like pizza—and who doesn't—a pizza stone is worth the investment (they're available at most cooking stores). A flat pizza paddle is also a help, although you can use a thin baking sheet in its place.

The recipe for this dough comes from Donna Scala of Ristorante Piatti in Yountville, California. I make it only with a mixer, but it can be done by hand. This dough recipe makes enough for three 8-inch pizzas. (You can freeze the extras.) The topping is enough for one pizza.

DOUGH

1¼ cups all-purpose flour
⅔ ounce (1 package) active dry yeast
1½ teaspoons salt
⅔ cup warm water
2 tablespoons olive oil
Cornmeal

TOPPING

½ cup chopped white onions
1 tablespoon unsalted butter
2 cups peeled, seeded, and chopped tomatoes
3 tablespoons minced fresh tarragon
¼ teaspoon salt
¼ teaspoon black pepper
3 tablespoons olive oil
¼ cup grated Parmesan cheese
2 ounces Romano cheese, shaved

Make the dough: Put the flour in the bowl of a stationary mixer fitted with a dough hook. In a small bowl, dissolve the yeast and salt in the water and allow to sit for a few minutes, until foamy. With the mixer at low speed, combine the yeast mixture with the flour. Add the olive oil and continue mixing. When the ingredients are well blended, increase the speed to medium and continue for 3 minutes. Switch back to low for another 3 minutes. Turn the dough out on a floured surface and cover with a damp towel. Let it rise for an hour.

Divide the dough into three equal balls. The dough should have a smooth and somewhat "tense" surface. Place each ball in a separate large plastic bag and seal. Refrigerate and allow to rise a second time overnight.

Put a pizza stone in the oven and sprinkle it lightly with cornmeal. Preheat the oven to 500 to 550 degrees.

Make the topping: Sauté the onions in the butter over medium heat, stirring, until browned, 6 to 8 minutes. Set aside.

Toss the tomatoes with the tarragon, salt, and pepper. Put in a colander and set aside in the sink to drain.

Meanwhile, roll out a ball of pizza dough into an 8- to 9-inch round. Sprinkle the pizza paddle or baking sheet lightly with cornmeal and transfer the dough to it. Turn up the edge, making a shallow rim all around. Sprinkle half the olive oil on the dough, brushing to cover evenly. Scatter the onions over this, and top with the grated Parmesan. Spoon on the tomatoes and spread evenly. Drizzle with the remaining oil.

Slide the pizza off the paddle onto the heated stone and bake until browned, 7 to 9 minutes. Remove and sprinkle with the shaved Romano. Cut into wedges and serve.

Serves 2

OVERLEAF: *Tomato Tarragon Pizza.*

SALADS

Everybody knows tomatoes can be made part of almost all salads that come out of the kitchen, but my favorites are the ones where tomatoes dominate.

TOMATO AND RED ONION WITH OLIVES AND ROMANO

———◆———

Like the salad of tomatoes and feta (see page 47), you don't need any recipe for this. All you do is peel and slice tomatoes and top them with slices of red onion. Spoon a little Strong Vinaigrette (page 47) over, and sprinkle with salt and a grind of black pepper. Finally, add "curls" of Romano cheese, made with a vegetable peeler. Garnish the salad with black olives.

TOMATO AND BREAD SALAD

———◆———

This recipe for *panzanella*, as it is known in Italy, comes from Hiro Sone, the very talented chef/owner of the restaurant Terra in St. Helena, California. Hiro's is, hands down, the best version of this Italian classic I know of.

When I make this, I make a double batch of croutons, toast them, and freeze half.

> *½ small baguette (about 12 inches long)*
> *1 large garlic clove, mashed*
> *Olive oil for brushing*
> *6 medium to large tomatoes, cut into large*
>   *chunks*
> *½ medium onion, chopped*
> *3 tablespoons coarsely chopped fresh basil*
> *4 tablespoons balsamic vinegar*
> *½ cup olive oil*

Preheat the oven to 300 degrees.

Split the baguette in half lengthwise. Rub the cut side of one half very well with the mashed garlic. Brush liberally with olive oil. Cut the garlicked half in half again lengthwise, and then cut these strips into ¾-inch pieces. Place the croutons on a baking sheet, crust side down. Bake 30 minutes, until dark golden.

If croutons are made in advance, put the tomatoes in a large mixing bowl a bit before you intend to mix the salad, then drain off and discard any juice that may accumulate.

To serve, add the croutons, onion, and basil to the tomatoes. Whisk together the vinegar and oil for the vinaigrette. Pour over all and toss.

Serves 6

TOMATOES AND LEMONS

The trick here is to slice the lemon *very* thin and to put the whole thing together about 30 minutes before you eat it, to give the salad time to marinate in the refrigerator. I'm not going to give you a recipe. Instead, take a look at the picture and arrange lemon slices alternating with tomato slices as shown. I take all the end slices of tomato, chop them, and heap them in a line along the middle of the dish.

Just before serving, sprinkle with salt and black pepper.

TOMATO SLICES WITH FETA AND CHOPPED HERBS

Cut tomatoes in half crosswise and fish out the seeds. Place on a platter and top with crumbled feta cheese. Sprinkle with minced chives and parsley, basil strips, salt, and freshly ground black pepper. Spoon Strong Vinaigrette over all.

STRONG VINAIGRETTE

1 teaspoon salt, or to taste
1 heaping teaspoon green-peppercorn mustard
Scant ½ teaspoon black pepper
2 tablespoons balsamic vinegar
3 tablespoons vegetable oil
2 to 3 tablespoons olive oil

Whisk all ingredients together.
Makes about ½ cup

OVERLEAF: *Tomato Slices with Feta and Chopped Herbs.*

TOMATOES WITH HONEY AND BLACK PEPPER

———◆———

Honey is a great complement to the flavor of tomatoes (tomatoes, you may remember, are technically fruits). To make this salad, peel a large tomato, cut it into thick slices, and spread each slice thinly with honey. Sprinkle the honeyed slices with salt and black pepper, then reassemble the tomato. Brush it lightly with more honey, and give it a sprinkle of salt and pepper. Refrigerate for about 20 minutes, and serve cool.

ALSAS

When did tomato salsa become so ubiquitous? I feel as if it's been around forever, but when I think back on it, this wonderful spicy concoction must have migrated east about the time California cooking started to take off. Bless them for it.

I think you can see from these two examples how subjective the ingredients and their quantities are. You start with tomato, onion, jalapeño pepper, salt, and black pepper—and you go on from there.

BASIC TOMATO SALSA

This recipe came to me from John Schmidt of those cookin' California Schmidts. He holds forth at the Booneville Hotel, which he owns and runs with his wife in Booneville, California. John says you can add either fresh oregano or mint to this.

> **2 cups diced ripe tomatoes**
> **½ to ¾ cup diced red onions**
> **3 to 4 large basil leaves, cut into thin strips**
> **Juice of 1 small orange**
> **1½ teaspoons balsamic vinegar**
> **½ jalapeño pepper, or to taste, seeded and**
> **   minced**
> **Salt and black pepper to taste**

Mix all ingredients together about 30 minutes before serving so the flavors will blend but still remain distinct.

Makes about 2½ cups

PEACH TOMATO SALSA

Here's a variation I often make.

> **2 cups diced ripe tomatoes**
> **½ cup diced yellow bell pepper**
> **1 cup diced peeled ripe peaches**
> **3 tablespoons seeded and minced jalapeño**
> ** pepper**
> **½ cup diced white onions**
> **3 tablespoons minced cilantro**
> **1 teaspoon salt**
> **3 tablespoons balsamic vinegar**

Mix all ingredients together and refrigerate, covered, for an hour. Allow to come back to room temperature before serving.

Makes about 3 cups

The truth is, I don't spend much time putting up any sort of preserves—especially not things that are so readily available in specialty stores. But sometimes I do make small batches of things that will keep reasonably well in the refrigerator.

FRESH TOMATO CHUTNEY

This is a very good addition to lamb or any other grilled meat. You can make it as hot or as mild as you like.

> *⅔ cup golden raisins*
> *½ cup fresh orange juice*
> *2 cups peeled, seeded, and chopped tomatoes*
> *5 green onions, minced (with some green)*
> *1 medium garlic clove, minced*
> *1 small red chili pepper (about 4 inches),*
> *   seeded and minced*
> *1½ tablespoons minced fresh ginger*
> *3 tablespoons minced cilantro*
> *1 to 1½ tablespoons fresh lime juice*
> *Salt to taste*

Put the raisins in a small nonreactive bowl and cover with the orange juice. Allow to sit for about 30 minutes. Drain, reserving the raisins and discarding the juice.

Toss the raisins with the remaining ingredients, and allow to marinate for about an hour before using.

Makes about 2½ cups

REFRIGERATOR YELLOW TOMATO PRESERVES

———◆———

I use yellow cherry tomatoes for this because they are less acid than the red ones; also, oddly enough, I like the crunch of their seeds in this. The recipe below is for the minimum amount you'd want to make. I usually double it.

> **1 pint yellow cherry tomatoes, peeled**
> **¼ cup water**
> **1½ cups sugar**
> **2 to 3 sticks cinnamon**
> **10 whole cloves**
> **1 bay leaf**
> **2 limes, thinly sliced**

Put the tomatoes in a nonreactive saucepan. Add the water and sugar. Bring to a boil over medium-low heat, and simmer until the sugar is dissolved, 2 to 3 minutes. Off the heat, add the cinnamon, cloves, and bay leaf. Cover and let sit at room temperature overnight.

Bring the mixture back to a boil. Remove the tomatoes with a slotted spoon and set them aside. Continue to boil the syrup slowly for about 15 minutes, or until thickened. Place the tomatoes and lime slices in a heat-resistant container, and pour the hot syrup over them. Allow to cool and refrigerate, tightly covered.

Makes 1½ to 2 cups

This is another one of those combinations where the ingredients really like one another.

MEXICAN EGGS

What this actually amounts to is scrambled eggs with salsa—so just scramble your eggs the way you like them and top with Basic Tomato Salsa (page 51).

A variation of this is to thin out the salsa with a bit of chicken stock and add a little more Tabasco to make it hotter. Heat this in a saucepan and poach the eggs in the liquid. *Then* top it with fresh salsa.

TOMATO SOUFFLE

This isn't exactly a diet dish, but it doesn't have egg yolks in it, and there's only a little butter and milk per serving. Whatever, it's great for lunch.

Sometimes the base isn't reduced properly, so the bottom of the soufflé ends up a little watery. This doesn't matter—it's just as good.

4 tablespoons unsalted butter
3 pounds tomatoes, coarsely chopped
1 tablespoon loosely packed minced tarragon
1 tablespoon tomato paste
3 tablespoons flour

1 cup milk
¼ cup freshly grated Parmesan cheese
¼ teaspoon black pepper
Salt to taste
5 egg whites
½ teaspoon cream of tartar

Preheat the oven to 350 degrees and prepare a 2-quart soufflé dish, or 6 to 8 individual soufflé dishes, by dusting inside with flour. Set aside.

Melt 1 tablespoon of the butter in a large skillet over medium heat. Add the tomatoes and tarragon and cook over medium-low heat for 40 minutes to reduce well. Stir occasionally to prevent sticking and scorching. Put through a food mill to strain out the seeds and skins. Be sure to press out as much pulp as possible before discarding the waste. Add the tomato paste to the reduced pulp and mix. Set aside until slightly cooled, about 15 minutes.

In the top of a double boiler, melt the remaining butter. Add the flour, mixing well, and cook for about 4 minutes, stirring. Whisk in the milk, making sure all lumps are dissolved. Cook until the sauce thickens. Add the tomato mixture and the cheese, and stir until it melts. Stir in the pepper and salt.

Beat the egg whites until foamy, add the cream of tartar, and beat until stiff but not dry. Stir a quarter of the beaten whites into the tomato mixture. Pour this over the remaining egg whites and fold in gently. Do not overmix; a few lumps are okay.

Pour into the soufflé dish and bake in the center of the oven for 30 minutes, until puffy and lightly browned on top.

Serves 6 to 8

OVERLEAF: ***Tomato Soufflé.***

PIPERADE PIE

◆

If you don't have a deep 10- or 11-inch pie pan, make two smaller pies. You could also cheat a bit and use two frozen 9-inch piecrusts. They won't have cheese in them, but you could always sprinkle a heaping tablespoon of grated Parmesan on top of each pie to make up for it.

Incidentally, the pastry recipe makes a large quantity, but I find that easier to work with. Ball up the scraps, roll them out, cut into strips, and bake them to eat along with drinks. Or refrigerate the leftovers and bake the strips later for a snack.

PASTRY

1½ cups flour
Pinch of salt
6 tablespoons unsalted butter, cut into bits and frozen
3 tablespoons solid shortening, frozen
1½ cups grated cheddar cheese
3 tablespoons ice water

FILLING

1¼ cups coarsely chopped red bell peppers
¾ cup coarsely chopped onions
6 tablespoons coarsely chopped green onions (with some top)
4½ tablespoons olive oil
1 tablespoon minced garlic
3 cups peeled, seeded, and chopped tomatoes
2 tablespoons coarsely chopped fresh basil

2 teaspoons salt, or to taste
1½ teaspoons black pepper
6 dashes Tabasco sauce
3 tablespoons unsalted butter, melted
6 large eggs, lightly beaten

Preheat the oven to 400 degrees.

Make the pastry: Mix the flour and salt. Cut in the butter, shortening, and cheese with a pastry blender or two knives until the mixture resembles coarse meal. Stir in the water, mixing well but quickly. (This may also be done in a food processor.) Form the pastry into a ball and flatten between two sheets of waxed paper. Refrigerate for 30 minutes.

Roll out on a lightly floured surface and line a deep 10- or 11-inch pie pan, crimping the edges and pricking with the tines of a fork. Then line the pan with foil. Cover the bottom with a layer of dried peas or pie weights. Bake for 15 minutes, until the pastry is set. Remove the weights and foil. Bake another 10 minutes, or until golden. Set aside to cool.

Make the filling: In a large skillet over medium heat, sauté the peppers, onions, and green onions in the olive oil until the vegetables are wilted, about 10 minutes. Stir in the garlic. Add the tomatoes, basil, salt, black pepper, and Tabasco. Bring to a slow simmer and continue cooking to reduce the liquid, about another 10 minutes. Remove from the heat and stir in the melted butter, then mix in the eggs.

Pour into the baked pie shell and bake for about 15 to 20 minutes, or until the filling is set but not dry.

Allow to rest for a few minutes to set before slicing.
Serves 8

OVERLEAF: *Pipérade Pie.*

You'll find lots of uses for these recipes . . . as vegetable toppings or tossed with pasta. The butters are especially good as sandwich spreads, and the vinaigrettes really complement fish.

SAVORY TOMATO BUTTER

¼ cup minced onion
½ cup (1 stick) unsalted butter, plus 2
   teaspoons
3 cups peeled and seeded tomatoes, pureed

Sauté the onion over medium heat in the 2 teaspoons of butter until it just begins to color, 3 to 4 minutes. Add the tomato puree and bring to a boil. Turn the heat down to a simmer and cook for about 5 minutes. Strain the mixture through a fine strainer, pressing to get out most of the liquid. Put the liquid in a clean saucepan. Bring to a boil over medium-low heat and cook, stirring occasionally, until reduced to 2 or 3 tablespoons, about 30 minutes. During the last 10 minutes or so, take care to keep it from scorching. Let it cool.

Beat the reduction into the remaining butter. Refrigerate until ready to use.

Makes about ¾ cup

SWEET AND TART TOMATO BUTTER

This recipe comes from painter Neil Welliver's mother, Mamie, who grew up in rural Pennsylvania. It's addictive! Use it for fruit sandwiches or breakfast toast.

> *8 large tomatoes, peeled*
> *1 cup sugar*
> *½ teaspoon salt*
> *1 teaspoon cinnamon*
> *2 whole cloves*
> *1 tablespoon fresh lemon juice*

Remove the seeds from half the tomatoes and chop the tomatoes coarsely. Measure out 4 cups of chopped tomatoes and put in a nonreactive saucepan. Mix in all the other ingredients. Simmer over very low heat, stirring occasionally to prevent scorching, until thickened and reduced to 2 cups, about 2 hours. When cool, cover tightly and refrigerate.

Makes 2 cups

TOMATO OIL

———◆———

You can gild the tomato by using this oil to dress tomato salad, with a good squeeze of lemon and a grind of black pepper.

> *3 pounds tomatoes, unpeeled but coarsely*
> *   chopped*
> *¼ cup good olive oil*
> *1 teaspoon minced fresh basil*
> *1 teaspoon minced fresh tarragon*

Put the tomatoes in a food processor and pulse a few times. Transfer to a strainer and press out all pulp and liquid. Discard the seeds and skins. Put the tomato pulp in a small saucepan over medium-high heat and reduce to 1 cup, about 30 minutes. Do not allow to scorch. Put it through the strainer again and return to the heat. Reduce to ½ cup, about 10 minutes. Mix in the olive oil and herbs. When cool, cover and refrigerate.

Makes about ¾ cup

OVERLEAF: *Tomato Oil.*

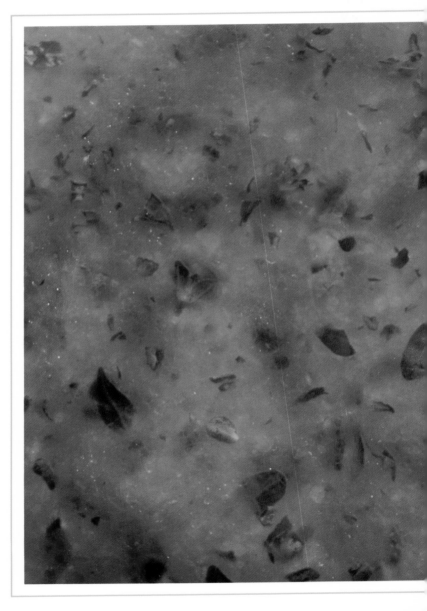

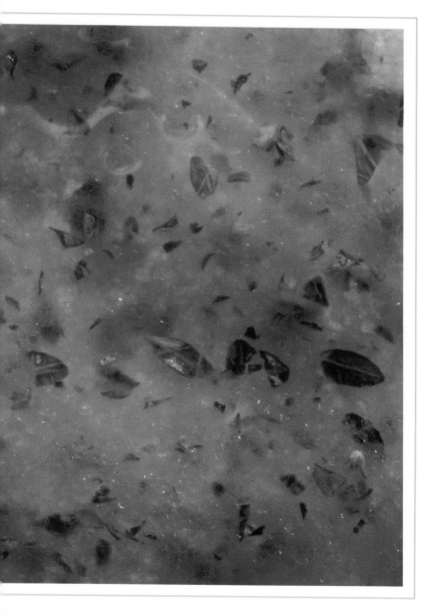

WARM TOMATO VINAIGRETTE

¼ cup olive oil
¼ cup minced shallots
1 cup peeled, seeded, and finely chopped
   tomatoes
¼ cup red wine vinegar
1 medium garlic clove, minced
⅔ cup dry white wine
¼ teaspoon salt
Black pepper to taste
2 tablespoons minced gherkins
3 tablespoons small capers, drained

Heat the oil and add the shallots. Cook over low heat until wilted, about 5 minutes. Do not brown. Add the tomatoes and simmer for 5 minutes. Add the vinegar, garlic, wine, salt, and pepper. Simmer for another 15 to 20 minutes, until reduced to a thick sauce. Correct the seasoning, and stir in the gherkins and capers.

Makes about 1½ cups

GREEN TOMATOES

This falls under the category of "If you can't beat 'em, join 'em." When I give someone a recipe for something that calls for green tomatoes and they ask, "Where can you get them?" I always say, "What do you think you are buying at every supermarket around?" Those pale (and even the gassed red) rocklike things you can buy out of season are all green—whether they are actually that color or not.

Of course, if you have a garden you can have the real thing when they're in season.

GREEN TOMATO AND APPLE PIE

Green tomatoes lend this pie a very distinctive flavor. I find that weighing the flour makes this more accurate.

10 ounces flour
1 tablespoon sugar
¼ teaspoon salt
3 tablespoons vegetable shortening, frozen
¾ cup (1½ sticks) unsalted butter, cut into small bits and frozen
6 tablespoons ice water

FILLING

1 cup sugar
¼ teaspoon salt
½ teaspoon cinnamon
1 tablespoon grated lemon zest
2 cups peeled, cored, and thinly sliced tart apples
2 cups thinly sliced green tomatoes, with any large seeds removed
1 tablespoon fresh lemon juice
½ cup (1 stick) unsalted butter
Heavy cream, flavored whipped cream, or ice cream

Make the pastry: Combine the flour, sugar, and salt in a food processor and pulse to mix. Add the vegetable shortening and pulse to mix lightly. Add half the butter and pulse several times just to chop slightly. Add the rest of the butter and pulse just long enough to mix coarsely. You should still be able to see pieces of butter. Sprinkle ice water over all and pulse just long enough for the pastry to start to cling together.

Gather the dough into a ball and divide in two. Place each half between sheets of waxed paper and flatten slightly. Wrap and refrigerate for about an hour.

Preheat the oven to 450 degrees.

Make the filling: Combine the sugar, salt, cinnamon, lemon zest, apples, and tomatoes in a bowl and toss well. Toss in the lemon juice.

Roll out one ball of pastry and line an 8-inch pie pan with it. Heap the tomato mixture in, mounding it slightly in the center. Dot with the butter.

Roll out the second ball of pastry and cut it into ½- to ¾-inch strips. Weave the strips into a lattice over the filled pie. Seal the edges and crimp.

Bake for 10 minutes, then turn the heat down to 350 degrees. Bake for another 35 minutes, until the crust is golden. Let cool on a rack.

Serve with cream, whipped cream, or ice cream.

Serves 8

OVERLEAF: **Green Tomato and Apple Pie.**

GREEN TOMATO RATATOUILLE

I like this served just warm or at room temperature. It's great to have in the summer.

>*6 tablespoons olive oil*
>*1 pound green tomatoes, very coarsely chopped*
>*1 large green bell pepper (approximately ½ pound), seeded and coarsely chopped*
>*3 very large garlic cloves, minced*
>*1 pound white onions, coarsely chopped*
>*1¾ pounds ripe tomatoes, coarsely chopped*
>*1 pound zucchini, cut into medium-thin rounds*
>*1 tablespoon salt*
>*1 teaspoon black pepper*
>*Pinch of crushed red pepper*
>*1 tablespoon minced fresh basil or ½ teaspoon dried basil*

Heat the oil in a large skillet and add the green tomatoes, bell pepper, garlic, and onions. Sauté, stirring lightly, until the vegetables are wilted, 7 to 8 minutes. Add the ripe tomatoes and zucchini. Cook until the zucchini is tender and the tomatoes have given up a lot of liquid. Add the seasonings and mix carefully. Continue to simmer at higher heat, stirring lightly, until most of the liquid has evaporated and what is left has thickened. Keep scraping from the bottom to keep it from scorching and sticking.

To serve hot, reheat in a double boiler.

Serves 6 to 8

CORNMEAL PAN-FRIED GREEN TOMATOES

These are great as a Sunday-morning treat with sausage. Some folks sprinkle them with sugar instead of salt and pepper.

> *Flour*
> *1 egg beaten with a little milk*
> *Yellow cornmeal*
> *¼-inch slices green tomato*
> *Oil for frying*
> *Salt and black pepper to taste*

Spread the flour on a sheet of waxed paper. Put the egg wash in a shallow dish. Spread the cornmeal on a sheet of waxed paper.

Dredge the tomato slices in flour and shake off the excess. Dip each slice in egg and drain off the excess. Coat with cornmeal, shaking off the excess lightly.

Heat the oil in a large heavy skillet over a medium flame. When hot, add the tomatoes. Cook several minutes, until golden, then turn. Sprinkle with salt and pepper.

TOMATO SANDWICHES

When I was growing up the tomato sandwich was roughly equivalent to chicken soup in my family—guaranteed to cure everything from bee stings to depression. So it seems appropriate to end with it. Tomato sandwiches are a snap to make, and if you are not already acquainted with their miraculous curative powers, it's time you gave yourself a treat—as well as a treatment.

There are two basic ones: the classic—which is made on nicely toasted bread spread with homemade mayonnaise—and the tomato tea sandwich—which is made on thin-sliced white bread (trimmed) spread with softened Tabasco butter (or plain). Nowadays, I often add a sprinkling of radish sprouts to the tea sandwich.

Of course, there's that great all-American favorite, the BLT, which probably began as the classic and got added to right after the first strip of bacon was fried.

I don't think I have to give you a recipe for making any of these. Luckily, we all seem born with the right instincts.